Do You Stop to See?

DO YOU STOP TO SEE?

Book of Poems Volume I

JANE PICARD
Xulon Press

Xulon Press
2301 Lucien Way #415
Maitland, FL 32751
407.339.4217
www.xulonpress.com

© 2018 by Jane Picard

All rights reserved solely by the author. The author guarantees all contents are original and do not infringe upon the legal rights of any other person or work. No part of this book may be reproduced in any form without the permission of the author. The views expressed in this book are not necessarily those of the publisher.

Scripture quotations taken from the New American Standard Bible (NASB). Copyright © 1960, 1962, 1963, 1968, 1971, 1972, 1973, 1975, 1977, 1995 by The Lockman Foundation. Used by permission. All rights reserved.

Scripture quotations taken from the New King James Version (NKJV). Copyright © 1982 by Thomas Nelson, Inc. Used by permission. All rights reserved.

Printed in the United States of America.

ISBN-13: 9781545620496

CONTENTS

PART I
THOUGHTS

Run, Run, Run
Winter Mystery
Trust
Shelter
Do We Stop to See?
It's What You Do
Day of Worship
Complementary
Pretending
Youth
Seconds
Knowing
Fake
Enough
You Knew
Storm
Untruth
Untruth- Short Version
Take a Minute
What Is It to Have?
Controversies

continued

viii | *Book of Poems Volume I*

Fact That You Are
Hunger Follows Me
See
Father
Mother
Brother
Word
OOPS!
Man Named Query
Wasted Time
Petal's Dance
Possibilities
Hurricane's End
MARVELOUS
Angels and Demons
Kingdom Inheritance
Autumn's Reminder
Best Friends Forever
Love for Israel
Violin
Haiti
Withered Tree
Light in Our Pain
Lullaby

Book of Poems Volume I | ix

PART II
HEARTS

Things We Do
Memory
Don't Forget
Start of Something
Together
John 3:16

Foreword

A foreword needs to capture and express the thought of the author succinctly. I am out of words to express the thoughts of this author in her book of poems, "Do You Stop to See?"

In her book of poems, Jane Picard expresses her life experiences, feelings and emotions and those that she's observed; in so many unique ways, to her readers that they would be elated. In almost an acoustic format, each word brings an expanded thought; her expressions bring you to the present, living the actual moment she described.

The author never failed to bring out her redeemer and sustainer- the All Mighty God. She describes God as the "I AM," the always present. Her description of God entices my desire to search for a closer relationship with The I AM.

This book, "Do You Stop to See?", depicted a heart that has been so many places, dealt with different facets of life. In my contention, every reader can find her/his place, whether it's hurt, perplexed, bruised, violated, blessed, admired, you name it, you can find it.

xii | *Book of Poems Volume I*

I would definitely recommend this book of poems to anyone, regardless of their social entourage. The book brings you closer to reality; enhances relationships by understanding people we interact with, and a reality check to ourselves. Reading this book will change your life!

Dr. Ted Ridoré

DEDICATION

This book is dedicated to my

GOD YHWH
Who sent His Son YESHUA so I could be free in
Him. I owe my life, and ability to dream to His
unending love for me. He is my Aleph, my Tev,
my Everything

FAMILY
My Dad, Jean Claude, who studied and sacri-
ficed so much so I could be where
I am today
My Mom, Lamercie, whose love, courage and
love of books inspires me
My Brother, Dean, who is so kind and dear
My Brother Danny
My Godfather, Herve Lamothe, and Godmother,
Geralda Lamothe, whose help
I'll never forget
My Uncle Joseph David and his family
All my Uncles and Aunts

FRIENDS
(No particular order)
To Lisa Graham my cheerleader and BFF, and her family
(Husband Rick, daughter Autumn)
To Pastor Ulrick Beauplan who challenges me to live for Christ, his wife Rosette
and his family
To Dr. Ted Ridoré my professor, an author and fellow nature enthusiast for teaching me you can when others say you can't, thank you so much
To Alice Lawson (and her family) whose love of French brought her into our family
as a friend
To Rosa Acampora whose talent with the violin is incredible
To Merri Bolen GS leader and a survivor
To Mae Dulae Martin and her family
To Dr. Serge E. L. Vernet a wise and Godly man who is a prolific author
To Dr. Limoné A. Joseph a true renaissance man and author
To Claudette Macey who is so supportive
To Ptr John (great singer/actor) & Ann Cavazos thanks for believing in me & my talent
Mr. Alwyn Morgan, Sr.
Ap. V. Parkerson
Glenette Bruce, Susanna Cunningham and All My Friends

OTHER

To Haiti, the Pearl of the Antilles, land where the poets hail from

To Chicago city of my youth, full of history, music, best pizza on the planet, sports, subways, culture, struggles, politics, art, fun and more

To the adventurers who risk to share their heart's pursuits in front of the world to see!

PART I
THOUGHTS
(and OBSERVATIONS)

Run, Run, Run

Run, Run, Run, but where?
Run to the hills,
But the hills are too high.
Run to the cities,
But they are too crowded.
Run home,
But you can never go home.
Run to Man,
But they're chasing their tails.
Run to the Oceans,
But I can't swim.

Stop, Stop, Stop, but Why?
For what you seek is within.
Stop, look within.
Within where?
Stop, look He who is within.
But who is within?
Stop, pray and call out
To Him who is Counselor, Friend, Savior…
Stop and call out to the Holy Spirit,
He who is everlasting to everlasting.

Peace, Peace, Peace, No questions needed.

Winter Mystery

Heart of winter the snowflakes fall,
Each unique,

I saw things wither far away,
Out of reach.

Could they come back I wonder,
Interestingly

Underground busy with activity,
A mystery.

Frozen in time but for a while,
First phase.

Hiding spring's glorious floral,
Array.

Trust

Trust

Assured, hopeful

Sterling, lying, crossing

Hard to regain once it is lost

Faith

Shelter

Where do I go?
Where do I hide?
Where is my shelter
From life's demise?

Is it in my smile
When things are rough?
Is it in my thoughts
That lift me up?

Where do I go
When evening draws near
And no light can be seen?
Where do I go
When my soul is quivering?
Where is my hope
In this my terrible hour?

Is it in my good deeds
Stacked pile-high in Heaven?
Is it in coins
Safe in a vault?

The answer my dear is
Nearer than you know.
It's here within thee
Where soul meets spirit,
Laughter brings joy,
Dance springs hope,
Praise defeats tears
And I AM covers thee,
With the tree only He could bear.

Go to the Cross
Go on bended knee.
Rest in His Victory.

Do We Stop to See?

Do we stop to see the trees how lovely God made them be?
All their gnarls and textured surfaces and all the moss upon its limbs,
Roots and all. How the squirrels run up its trunk for a nut.
Do we stop to see the man who stumbles on his feet?
Do we stop to see the sky how blue and true it is above?
Do we stop to see how beautiful God's world can be?
Or do we walk and walk along and just forget,
Blinded by it all, too busy to see, too fast to stop?

What causes our eyes to glance away
To never stop and say, "How wonderful and sweet,
How good and lovely is this day?"
Yet we clamor and complain and say,
"I wish I had another day, another life tomorrow come quick"
And yet have not fulfilled today's requirement to love and be.
So maybe next time as you go to and fro
You'll stop and say, "Today I'll *stop*, to *see*!"

It's What You Do

It's what you do for others
Which shines brightly heaven's love.
It's what brings them close
So they may see the light.

It's what you do for others
In a twinkle of an eye
Which brings angels 'round to cheer,
In such pure delight;
Wanting to place your deeds
In heaven's royal treasure chest.

It's what you do for others
In the quiet of the night
Or in the hustle and bustle of your day,
That shows you're not too busy
To stop and lend a hand.

It's what you do for others
That will be etched in the scrolls of time.
To one day be read aloud, a blessed testament.

Day of Worship

Sabbath

God's Holy Day

We worship, love and pray

Soul entwined joyfully with Him

Resting

Complementary

One and Two
> Is there a three?

A and B
> Do you C?

Red light, Green light
> A children's game.

Smile or Frown
> Your choice today.

Freedom and Chains
> One man's joy another's injustice.

Black and White...
> ...We're ALL Humans.

Pretending

Pretend to see
Pretend to know
Pretend to care
Pretend to love

Laugh,
Laugh,
Laugh,
Laugh, in your face they do

Wail,
Cry,
Cry,
Wail
All the way to their grave for Judgement Day

Youth

Youthful

Restless, playful

Dreaming, changing, finding

Its stay is exceedingly brief

Childhood

Seconds

90 Seconds to heat a bowl of soup
45 Seconds is all you need to cross the street please
30 Seconds to create over 60 million red blood cells
15 Seconds to survive in outer space without a space suit
2 Seconds to say yes to the love of your life
.3 Seconds to be in the presence of the Eternal to begin a new life!

Knowing

Knowing when to keep on going…
Knowing when to let go…
Knowing which to do,
Is the hardest thing of all.

Knowing that you succeeded…
Knowing that you failed…
Knowing losing can be winning and winning
can be losing,
Is what wisdom's all about.

Knowing when to speak…
Knowing when to hush…
Knowing when to utilize each,
Is like a master swordsman with his sword.

Knowing there is a I AM…
Knowing the Name I AM…
Knowing the History of I AM…
Is not the same as *Knowing* to reach out to
The Great I AM!

Fake

Smiles full of malice
that's what they're about.

Eyes full of darts
piercing through your heart.

Lies that are a plenty
like a tsunami.

Fake to the core
like a cheap Versace.

Enough

Enough is not enough for some today.
If one why not two, five, or twenty-five?
One car, one house, one song, one day.

One whole seems small when wrongly compared.
One large pizza, one whole pie, one full moon to light up the night sky;
One dance team, one computer to make one concert extravaganza.

One is less than two, but when two come together they become one whole.
One Father, one Son, one Holy Spirit- One God.
One Person many functions, yet complete in every way.

What joy it is to know enough is enough and live in "enough's" blessings!

You Knew

You knew me from before I was ever born.
You knew me from my mother's womb.
You knew who I'd be and yet you wanted me that
was the plan.
You helped me come to know who you are and I've
loved you since, and here I am Calling out to you.
And so I am asking you my King, Savior of my very
soul to help me, to help me.

You knew me before I was ever born.
You knew me in my mother's womb
And so I'm here. I'm here for you.
I've come to know your name and now I'm
worshiping you.
Is this part of the plan?
And still you want me. You knew what
I'd be and who I'd be,
And still you said you wanted me, and so I am here.

You who are the maker of my destiny, my life;
I'm before you, shape it.
Don't let me falter down away, but bring me up
close to you so I can be the one
That you designed me to be.
I need to walk in the plans you have for me so,

scroll, roll it out so I can see.
Guide me. Be my trailblazer, King of Kings
and Lord of Lords, .
So I can go follow you into my destiny that's
why I'm calling out to you.
There's no life if it is not in You my Precious King.
So I am here today to say…

You knew me before I was ever born.
You knew me in my mother's womb.
You knew what I'd be, who I'd be,
my ups and downs, my failures and successes.
You knew them all and still you said you
wanted me.
You died so I could live. Now I want you to
let that come to be.
I've seen it in the word of God. You were
there from the beginning of time.
So father time show me what it all means.
Because I know there is something there, For
you I know you got to know more than I ever
thought could be.
I want you to open my eyes. I need for you to
write my name in the Book of Life.
I want you to keep me with you because you're

continued

the first you're the last.
You're my Aleph, You're my very soul. You're the one that I follow through it all.
Heal me my Jehovah Rapha. Heal me Rapha and give me a life worth living.

You knew me before I was ever born.
You're the writer of my destiny.
Clear the path as you are my trail blazer and I shall follow Thee everywhere
That you clear for me. I know this journey
is filled with ups and downs and twists.
Some I know and some are just a mystery.
Here I stand watching life's tragedies.
I'm hoping that somewhere in it I can f
ind beauty, I can find glory,
Where you'll be, where you are. Don't walk away.
Don't walk away. Bring me close, Bring me
close to you. Keep me yes; Keep me yes on
my knees so I can hear
From you and know where I'm supposed to be, where to go. Know my life is all for You. All I need is a little help from you. Open my eyes and move my feet towards you.

Storm

My heart was leveled
as their walls fell down
My eyes swelled up
as their rivers rose up
Tears ran down my cheek
as mud fell down their hills
My heart skipped a beat
as F1s hit and missed dwellings
My prayers went to heaven
as turtle doves flew up in the sky
In hopes of a miracle of survivors to find.

Untruth

When truth is gone… mere pleasantries
When truth is fake… it becomes twisted
When truth is twisted… manipulation begins
When truth is manipulation… it is corrupted
When truth is corrupted… erosion sets in
When truth is eroded… we dance around emptiness
When there is emptiness… we are lost
When there is loss… cold hearts
When there is coldness… apathy lives
When there is apathy… nothing real exists
When there is nothing… delusion reigns
When there is delusion… love is false

Left with bribes, frustration, threats, anger,
control, divination… <u>falsehood</u>.

Untruth- Short Version

When truth is gone... pleasantries
When truth is fake... twisted
When truth is twisted... manipulation
When truth is manipulation... corruption
When truth is corrupted... erosion
When truth is eroded... emptiness
When there is emptiness... loss
When there is loss... coldness
When there is coldness... apathy
When there is apathy... unreal
When there is nothing... delusion
When there is delusion... love is false

Left with bribes, frustration, threats, anger,
control, divination... <u>falsehood</u>.

Take a Minute

Take a minute look to the past
See all the good see all the bad
Praise what is uplifting repent on what was destructive

Take a minute look to the future
See what can be
Walk into a life reborn
Bringing enthusiastic zeal
To reshape your life anew.

Take a minute look at your present
See that you're forgiven, see the open door
Know you're here living, full of promise, hope and dreams
A bridge between two worlds that only you can build.

What Is It to Have?

What is it to have eyes but look away.

What is it to have ears but won't hear.

What is it to have legs but never move.

What is it to have arms but aren't outstretched.

What is it to have logic but see one plus one is three.

What is it to have knowledge but miss-applied.

What is it to have justice but let the guilty free.

What is it to have freedom but let others
imprison thee.

What is it to have Christ but love the world
instead.

Controversies

Controversies and trials are the meat we should eat
But we run and hide from the faces we meet
In fear of defending the truth deep within.

The tongue, the sword to speak God's word
To defeat the enemies fiery darts.

But instead the tongue is still, locked up in a vault
Of powerless fear adding a nail to freedom's coffin.

How shall we win? How shall justice prevail if we
The liberators lay down our arms watching injustice,
Hatred and SIN scurry on by?

Fact That You Are

The fact that you see it makes you connected.
The fact that you're connected makes you important.
The fact that you're important makes you impactful.
The fact that you're impactful makes you useful.
The fact that you're useful makes you resourceful.
The fact that you're resourceful makes you thoughtful.
The fact that you're thoughtful makes you delightful!

Hunger Follows Me

Hunger follows me walking all the way

Hunger follows me looking for a meal

Hunger sees my name selfish, unaware

Hunger questions me hopefully

Hunger follows me crying as it walks away

Hunger follows me no more.

See

I looked upon the sea and wondered what I'd see.
Wave after wave was all that came to me.
My heart was sad to think no special sight I'd see.

I looked upon the sea a second time and wondered what I'd missed.
Wave after wave was all that came to me.
But I was blinded by my eyes you see.

I looked upon the sea a third time and I saw Thee.
Wave after wave of love was what came to me.
My heart was glad for I saw glory engulf me.

I looked upon the sea and knew
Wave after wave it was You.
My eternal King reminding me,
Be still and know that I am near.

Father

Father found more than one thousand
times in the good Book
Is a needed thing to keep one on track
on the road of life
Teacher of law to his household abode
He is more than the exterior of muscles and bones
He is resourceful, encouraging, funny, and smart
A man known to all in his community for good
A man respected and loved by his wife and children
From Humble beginnings to entrepreneur
Blood in his veins from the land of the poets,
Jérémie
A Father is light when he lives in God's word
His love for his family cannot be erased
A giver, a friend, a renaissance man
Is my father to me.

Mother

She is strong, sweet, and sublime
First hug, first kiss, first teacher of mine
Respected, revered by all the children she reared
Loved by her husband all these years
Face of an angel, voice like thunder when upset
Daughter of Miragoâne, so lovely a place
Accountant, nurse, professor, police, lawyer, judge,
Plumber, gardener, chef, seamstress, painter,
Librarian… are just a few of the positions she holds
A proverbs woman could learn a lesson or two
from her
Friend as I grow older
Example of true courage and faith
Hands of compassion, heart full of love
No one but Christ could ever come closer
To the love of my mother.

Brother

Brother

Mother's baby

Friend, teasing, protecting

Father's male child, son - keeps his name

Sibling

Word

Word

Living

Eternal

Sweet as honey

It is a sharp sword

Rhema

OOPS!

Crash

    Boom,

        Oops!

Apologize.

Crash,

    Boom,

        Oops!

Apologize.

Crash,

    Boom,

        Oops!

        Enough is Enough, REPENT.

Man Named Query

There once was a man named Query,
Who loved to go and see the canaries.
One day he met Contrary,
Who said bye, bye you birdies.
They married,
Then fussed and complained daily.

Now they are both buried.

Wasted Time

Wasting time listening to you - bunch of lies
Wasting time defending you - reputation stained
Wasting time fighting for you - deep in the pit
Wasted time… I cannot get back.

Petal's Dance

Golden pedal falling down
gently dancing with the wind
until it reaches the fair ground.

It calls upon the others high
to join its sweet and glorious decent down.

A petal of golden brown;
one of green is rare to see.

This season is but the dance
of the Autumn leaves;
for evergreens know not this dance.

Possibilities

Possibilities are the name of the game
When you're living in faith
That's how it has to be.

If you'd only open up the eyes of your heart
You'd know that the greatest gift is love
For fear can't stay within its box.
And hope the key to unlock the power within.

Possibilities are the name of the game
When you're living in faith
That's how it has to be.

Hurricane's End

I stand among empty classroom desks that once
were filled with eager minds.
These were to be our future's best,
but all I see are empty desks.
Yellow, blue, and red ones eerily starring back.

Gone are the quarrelsome debates and
perplexing looks, and aha grins.
Where have all those longing, thirsty to
learn gone?

Did we fail to show them the key to a brighter day?
Did they sense there was no hope?
Or was it the atmosphere that choked it all?

But if you delve closer still you'll realize the
quiet stillness that I speak,
As the stench of death rising up my nostrils.
If you could see the lace of a pink tennis shoe,

bloodied on the broken, debris-speckled floor,
And better yet, as I turn to place my hand
upon the wall that is no more;

Keeps the secret of that day when winds
blew hard and people fled

In hopes it would protect them all.
You'd begin to know I saw the past in today's
mishap, Glory's past in today's sorrow.

*Please continue to pray for and help the people of Haiti who
have suffered so much from Hurricane Matthew.*

MARVELOUS

Maker
Artist
Redeemer
Victorious
Exquisite
Love
Omniscient
Unique
Supreme

Is my King to me!

Angels and Demons

Angels and Demons watching us,

Angels helping us, demons fighting us.

The redeemed with the power of His blood do win,

Entering God's eternal Kingdom.

Kingdom Inheritance

Did you ever stop to think
That you and I are
The apple of God's eye?

Born for greater things;
A royal priesthood
To judge and rule.

A kingdom gift from the true King,
Who saw not my iniquities
But future possibilities.

He so loved the clay
He made that day,
Though betrayed.

Positioned His royal scepter pardoning me,
By washing all my sins and tears
With His sacrificial blood.

Chains and garments stained with sin
Exchanged for freedom and white gowns
So I may dance, sing and worship Him.

Master of my heart and life,
Father to the fatherless,
Friend to those who are alone.

Wisdom, knowledge, faith, healing,
Miracles, mercy, love… are gifts
More precious than rubies or pearls.

I joyously await to rule
Beside my warrior King,
For those thousand years and all eternity!

Autumn's Reminder

Clean and crisp air blowing through my hair
First day of Autumn I do gather.
Snap chats and tweets announce its coming,
To all those eager to enjoy it!

Candy corn, pumpkins and leaves of many colors
Remind me of falls full delights:
Treats to come, thanks to give and beauty
in our midst!

Autumns of the world do chatter
Of the names their mothers garnered,
Celebrities of the moment; which bears their
name if not their likeness.
How sweet to be an *Autumn-* for a season!

The winds will grow,
The trees go bare,
In preparation for winter's soon approach!

Yet let us feast and thank the Lord for His great
bounty,
As the season calls us to.
For truly these are the signs to celebrate
Royalty's soon glorious arrival!

Best Friends Forever

I have known you forever; at least that's how it feels,
First glance, first words, so familiar to me.

Hoosiers and Bulls,
Piano and violin,
Pizza and beer, "oops root beer",
are the things we adore.

Spring and fall are the seasons of our birth.
Sisters in Christ
Though different in stature and appearance,
No one can tell us apart.

We laugh, cry and pray in one breath it appears.
No trial I could face without you by my side,
Oil and perfume make a heart glad,
So a man's counsel is sweet to his friend
(Proverbs 27:9 NASB)
I'm so blessed God sent you my
BEST FRIEND FOREVER!

Love for Israel

Oh thy Israel,
how I hope to see thy gates,
see thy walls and pray to YHWH.

Oh thy Israel,
first born of nations,
mighty in battle, strong in faith;
the apple of YHWH's eye.

Oh thy Israel,
capital of the world to come
stand by your redeemer,
your messiah, true King.
For the promises He made
is why I pray for thee.

Oh thy Israel,
I born gentile have come
to love thy King Yeshua;
who walked your streets,
dined in your homes,
laughed with your children,
healed your sick,
and died on a hill
so I may be FREE to worship He,
mighty King of Everything.

Violin

Violin Sings

Divinely Rhythmically

My Soul Uplifted!

Haiti

History's warriors of freedom in the Caribbean,
Art, soccer, music and food are some of the
things to enjoy,
Island paradise, *Pearl of the Antilles*,
full of beauty and strength,
Taíno, African, French, Polish, Asian… and more
in our veins,
In Heaven's hands you are left to shape
and to bless.

Withered Tree

To sit beside a withered tree and believe it's like me
scarred and gnarled, branches bended low
soon to be no more. Yet life exists upon its limbs
with new green leaves due to spring's new growth.

How sad this tree must have been had not
spring's grace
brought forth promise of new life upon its limbs.
Could life so share a promise as this for me?
Could life be springing too upon me,
but I can't see?
If death has not claimed me,
then life must reign within,
like this withered tree.

I am young but life has made me
as this withered tree.
And still I breathe, walk… and live!
Should nature be more blessed than me or
Am I to partake in spring's true abundance too?
Knowing He who made the tree and all the seasons
has called me out of winter's harsh trials too.
His sweet renewal when I pause to reflect on the
tree from long ago

continued

that held my Savior.
Eyes did too see a horrid thing, but hope
sprung eternal three days hence.

I now see, with hopeful eyes; I too am blessed
more than this withered tree.
For I can speak, praise and worship He who is
the King of the earth and universe.

Light in Our Pain

In the darkness

      of our
        pain,

We need a light,

           a light

               that can bring

truth

In truth comes breakthrough.

Lullaby

Head on my chest
Sweet baby's breath

I watch you sleep
So effortlessly

Fingers you curl
Upon my own

Gently I rock you
To sleep

In my arms
You will be.

PART II
HEARTS

Inspired by the love I've seen of my

Parents

Married Friends

and In The Word of God

Art work by Mrs. Geralda Lamothe an extrordinary painter.

Things We Do

The things that I do,
The things that I believe,
The things that I love,
The God that I serve,
Were there before I knew you;
Shaped and formed the person before you.

The things that you do,
The things that you believe,
The things that you love,
The God that you serve,
Were there before you knew me.

Then I met you.
The things that you do
I've come to do
The things that you love
I've come to love.

Now the things that we do,
The things that we believe,
The things that we love
The God that we serve,
Make me a better me,
You a better you and
Us a better We!

Memory

Early I awake glancing your handsome face
To my surprise you stir and look my way
Smiling eyes with a playful grin
Oh my! What's on your mind?!

Quickly I rise now that I'm caught
Yet no escape is found for me
Left or right each move is met with a kiss
What will I do? I must begin the day.

Gently you pull me close to you
Arms strong as steel, heart full of joy
Can this be real or am I dreaming still?

Tenderly you caress me
A torch within my heart ablaze
Fanned by your love it fiercely grows
How much I do not know?

Kindly you play with all of me
My hair, hands, twin peaks and thighs
Wondering will you make it to the garden of delight?

Happily we laugh and sing enjoying life's bounty
The rain upon your head and mine,
The sun, the moon, the stars cleverly
arranged for us
How can we make this moment last?

Warmly you answer, "By our daily memories"
Each kiss, hug, and moment can last
Since we are joined in His Heavenly embrace
For God so beautifully designed.

Don't Forget

You forgot love's first kiss that brings me near
You forgot the touch, the feel of my loving embrace
You forgot the laughter of my voice
You forgot the glow within my heart as I held
our children sweetly
You forgot the times we fought but then made up
You forgot the look you gave, full of admiration
You forgot the times I helped you and you me
You forgot how I sacrificed to help your family
You forgot all the wondrous holidays we
spent happily
You forgot all the times we prayed and
worshiped God together…

You forgot to forgive my deeds as God
commanded you to do
You forgot to fight for me, and let satan blind you
of my love for you…

I will not forget that love,
I will not forget to fight for us,
I will not forget that command to love you always,
Knowing love exists waiting to be freed from
forgetfulness.

Start of Something

It is the start of something great.
It is the start of something wonderful.
I will not stop. I will keep my heart looking forward.
It is the start of something great.
It is the start of something wonderful.
It is the start of life.

It is the start of where we are to be, to be
together as one.
It is the start of something wonderful don't you
feel it in the depths of your heart.
And what we do is shout out into the outerlands
and let the Lord hear our cry,
Our cry of joy, our cry of Love, our C—R—-Y!

And let him know this is the start of something
wonderful, something beautiful.
We don't know where we'll be, just that we
know that He is with us.
As we walk each and every day with
the hopes of it being sweet.

We all have our ups and downs.
But not today for we are high up, up, up.

continued

Us together oh yes.
I'm telling you the truth. Everything will be all
right if we just have faith and
Let it be in His mighty hands.
It is the start of something beautiful,
Oh yes the start of something great, the start of
something W-o-n-d-e-r-f-u-l.

Together

When you're in a jam and looking for someone
Well honey here I am, here I am.
Honey know, you know that God made me for you
He did, yes you do.
You know that I'm your love, I'm your heart
I'll have your back I do, I do, I do.
So when you're looking 'round trying to find your way
I will help you, yes I will.
I'll help you find it 'cause I'm following the light of truth
His name is Christ.
So I know Christ won't steer me wrong
So if we need some help I'll go to Him.
And then we won't be lost
No we'll always find the North Star,
the North Star.
'Cause my heart, my GPS is geared to Him
There's nobody else no, no, no
Just Jesus Christ and you, we'll conquer all the world for Him,
Just give us the plan.

John 3:16

I thank Thee
who saved me
according to
John 3:16

*For God So Loved the world that He gave His only
begotten Son, that whoever believes in Him should not
perish but have everlasting life.
John 3:16 NKJV*

About the Author

Jane Picard lives in Orlando, Florida. Family and friends are a precious part of her life. Her work with missions extends over 20 years. Currently Jane is involved in missions with Greater Calling Outreach (GCO) and the Haitian Self-Help Organization (HASHO). The chance to grow spiritually as a member of Breaking Bread Fellowship (BBF) is quite rewarding. She enjoys gardening, herbology, art, cooking, music, sports, the outdoors, making natural soaps, traveling, photography, reading and simply enjoying life's simple pleasures.

Jane Picard - janepicard7@gmail.com
https://janepicard7.wixsite.com/janepicardauthor

Greater Calling Outreach (GCO)
YouTube Channel: Greater Calling Outreach- GCO
Email: greatercallingoutreach@gmail.com

HASHO, Inc.
www.hashoinc.wixsite.com/hasho
Email: hashoi.org@gmail.com

YouTube Channel: Controversial Truth with Dr. Ted Ridore
Email: controversialtruthridore@gmail.com